$$mc^2$$

$$\varepsilon_0 = 8.85418782 * 10^{-12}$$

$$N_A = 6.022045 * 10^{23} \ mol^{-1}$$

$$E_1 + E_1 = E_1^2$$

DISCOVER
PHYSICS

Predominant artwork & imagery source:
Shutterstock.com

Copyright: North Parade Publishing Ltd.

4 North Parade,

Bath,

BA1 1LF, UK

This edition ©2020

Printed in China.

Contents

Energy

Energy, in simple terms, is the ability to do work. Energy is everywhere around us and is responsible for changes, chemical reactions, biological activity, and movement happening everywhere. Energy can also take up many different forms. Energy is measured in standard units called joules.

Energy System

A system is a group of objects. When there is any change in the system, the energy stored in one or more object in it also undergoes changes. Heat, force, electricity, and work can result in a change in an energy system. A few common examples include:

A ball hit by a bat

Boiling water in a kettle

A rock thrown up in the air

Types of Energy

All objects possess internal energy. Energy is primarily classified into potential and kinetic energy. Potential energy is stored energy. Kinetic energy is the result of movement. A rock lying on the ground might look like it does not possess energy. However, it contains stored energy known as potential energy. A moving object possesses kinetic energy as a result of the force that set it into motion.

The ability to transfer energy from one form to another has driven and continues to enable life on our planet. Plants and certain other organisms absorb energy from the Sun and convert it into food in the form of chemical energy. Organisms that consume them gain energy for their activities. Energy is never transferred wholly from one system to another. There is always wastage in the form of heat, light, or other forms.

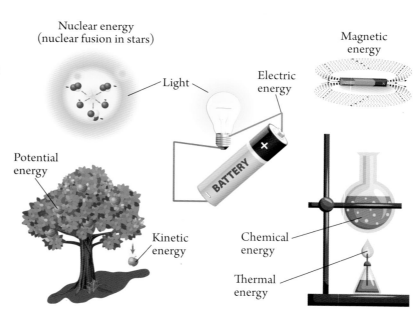

Nuclear energy (nuclear fusion in stars)

Magnetic energy

Light

Electric energy

Potential energy

Kinetic energy

Chemical energy

Thermal energy

▲ *Energy comes in different forms and can be transformed from one form to another.*

There are many forms of energy we can observe around us. The Sun is a source of light and heat energy. Nuclear energy is derived from the nuclei of atoms. Energy in magnets is magnetic energy, and energy in electric materials is electric energy. Chemical energy is stored in fuels, food, and batteries. Vibrating objects can produce sound energy.

Law of Conservation of Energy

Energy can neither be created nor destroyed. It can be stored or transferred from one form to another. Before and after transfer, the total energy in a system remains constant. An example of energy transfer is the heat radiating from a hot object to a cold object that comes into contact with it. This type of energy transfer is known as conduction.

▶ *The transfer of energy from a hot to cold body is called conduction.*

Potential Energy Due to Gravity

As the name suggests, the Earth's gravitational field exerts a pull on all objects, and the potential energy arising from it is the gravitational potential energy. A rock or any object located on top of a hill has gravitational potential energy. This is because, at some point in time, an external force must have been applied to enable it to gain that height.

A simple formula is used for calculating the energy of the object:

$$E = m\,g\,h$$

m – mass of the object
g – gravitational field strength
h – height from base of hill or raised structure

Fact File

Thrilling rides in theme parks work on the principle of transfer of gravitational potential energy to kinetic energy and vice versa.

▲ *In a roller coaster ride, there is a constant transformation from gravitational potential energy to kinetic energy.*

Power

The rate at which energy is transferred is called power. Alternatively, power can also be defined as the rate at which work is done. Power is measured in watts. A transfer of energy equivalent to 1 joule per second is equal to the power of 1 watt. The power of light bulbs is measured in watts e.g. 10W, 50W or 100W. The number (in watts) indicates the amount of power the bulb would consume in one hour.

▲ *The power consumed by a bulb is measured in watts.*

Energy Efficiency

No matter how effectively a system is designed to store energy, a certain amount of energy still dissipates into the atmosphere and gets wasted. Constant innovations help design energy-efficient systems that provide maximum utilisation of the stored energy and minimal wastage.

Energy efficiency is calculated using this simple formula:

$$\text{Efficiency} = \frac{\text{Useful Output Energy}}{\text{Total Input Energy}}$$

Energy Resources

The energy resources that are available on Earth for our use include fossil fuels like coal and petroleum, biofuel, nuclear energy from radioactive elements, hydroelectricity from running water, wind energy, tidal energy from waves, solar energy from the Sun and geothermal energy from Earth's internal heat. The energy harvested from different sources is used for electricity generation, heating and transport.

▲ *Coal is a fossil fuel that is burnt for generating energy.*

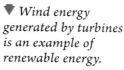

◀ *Solar panels harvest energy from the sun for heating purposes and powering appliances*

▼ *Wind energy generated by turbines is an example of renewable energy.*

▲ *Petrol and diesel that power vehicles are rapidly diminishing resources.*

Not all forms of energy can be replenished. Fossil fuels are an example of nonrenewable resources. They are available in limited quantities and might not even last this century. On the other hand, solar energy is renewable as the source, the Sun, will exist for billions of years. Renewable energy sources are a better option, because most of them (solar, wind and hydrothermal energy) are also nonpolluting.

Efficiency of Different Energy Sources

At a time when many energy sources are fast diminishing, researchers across the world are trying to identify better ways to harvest and store energy. One of the most important things to be kept in mind is the energy efficiency. It is important that a large portion of an energy source or fuel should be converted into energy with minimal wastage.

While comparing different fuels and sources, wind energy is considered to be the most energy efficient. Hydroelectric power is the least polluting, in terms of carbon dioxide released into the atmosphere. On the other hand, fossil fuels like coal and oil are the least efficient, providing as little as only 30 percent energy yield. Also, the burning of fossil fuels causes pollution, so it is necessary to replace them with better sources.

Not all places in the world can harvest wind for energy production. However, different places in the world take advantage of the available physical resources and climate patterns to produce energy. At present, the cost of solar panels used for harvesting energy from the Sun is quite high. With better innovations, the cost can come down and efficiency increased. Identifying newer ways for harvesting energy is necessary for meeting the demands of a growing world population.

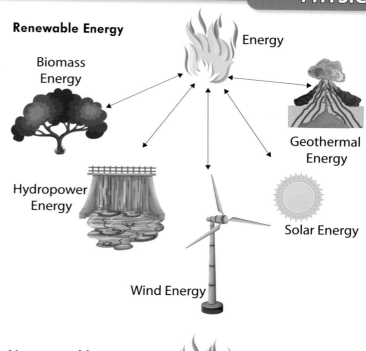

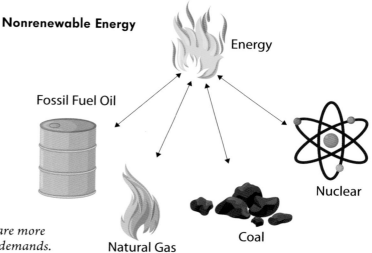

▶ *Renewable energy sources are more suitable for long-term energy demands.*

ENERGY EFFICIENCY

Percentage of energy input retained when converting fuel to electricity

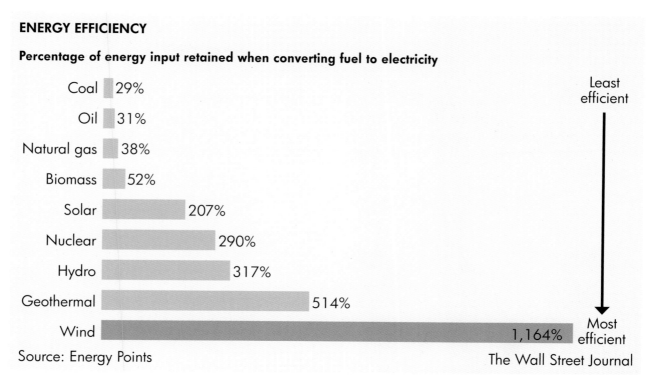

Coal 29%
Oil 31%
Natural gas 38%
Biomass 52%
Solar 207%
Nuclear 290%
Hydro 317%
Geothermal 514%
Wind 1,164%

Least efficient
Most efficient

Source: Energy Points

The Wall Street Journal

Structure of Atoms

Radioactivity, the ability of the nuclei of certain atoms to naturally disintegrate and emit ionising radiation, was discovered a long time ago. However, the structure and properties of atoms are known to us only recently. The knowledge of atoms' constituents has greatly advanced our knowledge and innovation in many fields.

Size of an Atom

An atom is minuscule, with a radius of about 1 angstrom. A heavy atom might have a radius of about 5 angstroms. An angstrom is 1×10^{-10} metres. For comparison, a grain of sugar is about 1 millimetre. A millimetre is 1×10^{-3} metres. An atom is 1/10,000,000 the size of the sugar granule. So, about 10 million atoms can fit into the space of a single grain of sugar.

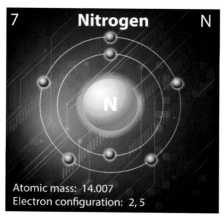

7   **Nitrogen**   N

Atomic mass: 14.007
Electron configuration: 2, 5

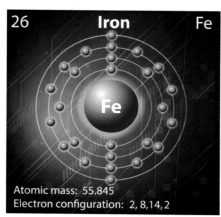

26   **Iron**   Fe

Atomic mass: 55.845
Electron configuration: 2, 8, 14, 2

▲ *Atoms can vary in size from 1 - 5 angstroms*

Atom Structure

An atom is the most basic particle of an element. It consists of a nucleus surrounded by electrons. An atom is small, but the nucleus is much smaller, with a radius of about 1/10,000 the size of an atom.

The nucleus consists of protons and neutrons. Negatively charged electrons, equal to the number of protons in the nucleus, are arranged at different distances around the nucleus. These distances are definite and are known as 'energy levels' or 'shells.' Electrons can move from one energy level to another by emitting or absorbing energy from the surroundings.

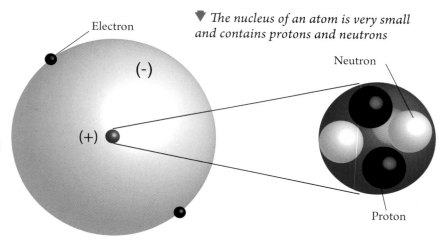

Electron

▼ *The nucleus of an atom is very small and contains protons and neutrons*

Neutron

(-)

(+)

Proton

An electron can be 'excited' by providing high voltage or energy to move from its original energy level to a higher energy level. However, an electron does not stay in the excited level for long, because all electrons like to stay in a shell that provides stability, known as a relaxed state. So, they release the excess energy in the form of light as they return to their old shell. An atom can become an ion by losing or gaining electrons.

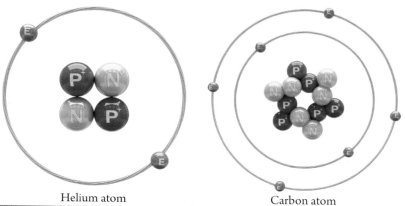

Helium atom   Carbon atom

A helium atom with two electrons in its only shell is stable because it has achieved maximum stability for that orbital. The electrons are said to be in a stable or relaxed state and helium is referred to as an inert gas.

A carbon atom has a total of six electrons, with two electrons in the innermost shell and four electrons in the next shell, with a maximum capacity of eight. Since it's only half-filled, carbon interacts readily with other elements.

In a series circuit, the same current passes through each component and the total potential difference across the circuit is shared between the components.

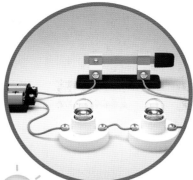

In a parallel circuit, the potential difference across each component is the same. The total current passing through the entire circuit is the sum of the currents through individual components.

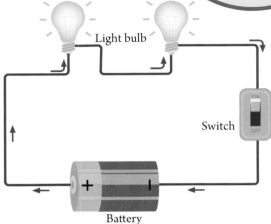

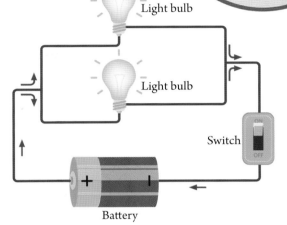

Domestic Electric Supply

The electric supply of the main unit is alternative current with a voltage of 230V. The electrical appliances are attached to the main supply through a three-core cable that can be plugged into a power socket.

The outer part of the wire is surrounded by an insulation material like plastic or rubber. The insulation covering each type of wire is colour-coded for easy identification. Live wire has brown insulation, neutral wire blue, and earth wire has green and yellow stripes. The live wire is the one that carries the alternating current from the main supply. The neutral wire completes the circuit. The earth wire is for appliance safety purposes. In case there is a fault in the electrical supply, the earth wire provides a path back for the electric current to flow harmlessly. In the absence of an earth wire, a person can receive a severe electric shock when touching an appliance.

▲ *Appliances are powered or charged by connecting a cable to a power socket.*

Power Grids

A power grid is a high-voltage power transmission network system that connects power stations and substations across a country. Power stations are equipped with transformers and electric cables that transfer power from stations to homes, workplaces, factories, and other buildings in the area. A transformer is useful for increasing or decreasing potential difference transmitted from power stations through cables.

➡ *Power stations and substations transfer power to all houses and factories in their vicinity.*

Nuclear Radiation

The nucleus of an atom consists of the protons and neutrons surrounded by an electron cloud. Almost the entire mass of the atom is concentrated in the nucleus. The nuclei of certain heavy atoms are unstable and emit radiation to achieve stability. This process is known as radioactive decay.

Radioactivity

Generally, it is the electrons of atoms that interact with each other and result in different reactions and form molecules. The nuclei of small atoms are more or less stable. The stability of a nucleus is determined by the number of protons and neutrons in it. In heavy atoms, there are many protons and neutrons. Since all protons are positively charged, the binding energy of the nucleus that holds together the protons and neutrons in the small space is not enough.

Electron

Neutron

Protons

(+) Protons
(●) Neutron ⎫
           ⎬ Nucleus
(-) Electron ⎭

▲ Though the nucleus is tiny, all the mass of an atom is concentrated here.

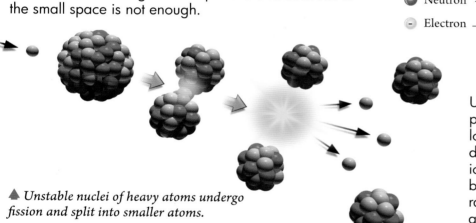

▲ Unstable nuclei of heavy atoms undergo fission and split into smaller atoms.

Unstable nuclei usually have excess protons and neutrons and try to lose them to achieve stability. The decay of the nuclei by emitting ionising radiation (such as alpha, beta, or gamma rays) is known as radioactivity. It is measured at the rate at which the unstable nuclei decay.

Ionising Radiation

When unstable nuclei decay, the radiation emitted is one of the three kinds: alpha or beta particles, or gamma rays.

Alpha particles: Each alpha particle consists of two neutrons and two protons and is similar to the nucleus of a helium atom.

Beta particles: A beta particle consists of a high-speed electron emitted from the nucleus when a neutron turns into a proton.

Gamma rays: Unlike alpha and beta particles, gamma rays are merely a release of energy from the nucleus to stabilise it. The release of gamma rays is almost always followed by the emission of an alpha or beta particle.

Any emission of ionising radiation changes the structure of the nucleus, and as a result the physical and chemical properties of the element. This phenomenon is known as transmutation of matter.

▼ Penetrating power of various types of radiation: comparison of penetrating ability of alpha, beta, and neutron particles, and gamma rays and X-rays

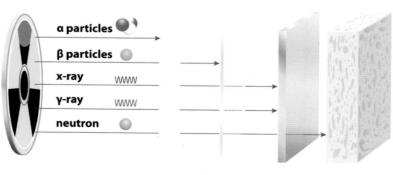

α particles
β particles
x-ray www
γ-ray www
neutron

Paper   Aluminium   Lead   Concrete
         plate

Radioactive decay is represented as nuclear equations. The emission of different types of radiation from the nucleus can have different effects. Alpha particle decay results in a change in the mass and charge of the nucleus—that is, both the mass and charge decrease. Beta particle decay does not affect the nucleus's mass, but increases the charge of the nucleus. Gamma ray emission does not change the charge or the mass of the nucleus.

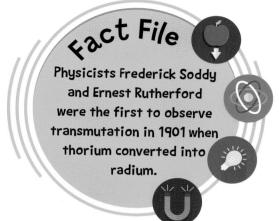

Fact File

Physicists Frederick Soddy and Ernest Rutherford were the first to observe transmutation in 1901 when thorium converted into radium.

▲ *Radioactive isotopes are stored in specially designed containers with warning labels.*

Half-Life of Radioactive Elements

Radioactive elements are those elements that are capable of undergoing radioactive decay. The half-life of an isotope of a radioactive element is the time taken for the decay of half the number of atoms in a sample.

For example, consider barium-139, which has a half-life of 86 minutes. If you have 100 grams of barium-139, after 86 minutes, 50 grams of the sample would have decayed and converted into another element. After another 86 minutes, you will observe that you are left with only 25 grams of the original sample. This goes on continuously until virtually all the atoms of barium-139 have decayed and converted into another element.

Different radioactive isotopes have different half-lives. Polonium-215 has an extremely short half-life of about 0.0018 seconds, making it very unstable. On the other hand, uranium-238 has a half-life of 4.5 billion years. Radioactive isotopes are stored in containers with a specific symbol to indicate that they have to be handled with caution.

Radiocarbon dating is a procedure that uses a particular isotope of carbon, carbon-14, with a half-life of 5,730 years. It is useful for identifying the age of ancient artifacts and fossils that are less than 40,000 years old. For identifying age of older specimens, uranium isotopes (which have longer half-lives) are used.

◀ *Radiocarbon dating is one useful application of radioactive isotopes.*

Nuclear Fission and Fusion

Nuclear fission is the process by which the large and unstable nucleus of a heavy atom such as uranium is split into smaller nuclei. Nuclear fission occurs when an unstable nucleus absorbs a neutron. It is very rare for nuclear fission to occur spontaneously. The nucleus undergoing fission splits roughly into two equally sized nuclei and releases about two or three neutrons and gamma rays. Tremendous amounts of energy are also released during the nuclear fission process.

Since the products of a fission reaction possess kinetic energy, the neutrons usually start a chain reaction. This chain reaction can be designed to occur in a controlled manner inside a nuclear reactor to harvest the energy produced for electricity generation. Uncontrolled nuclear fission chain reaction causes massive explosion and widespread damage, as in the case of nuclear weapons.

Nuclear fusion is the opposite of fission and is the process by which two light nuclei fuse together to form a heavy nucleus. This process results in the conversion of mass into energy and radiation. Nuclear fusion occurs continuously in the Sun.

Much of the energy generated by the Sun is the result of nuclear fusion of hydrogen nuclei into helium, continuously. About 620 million metric tons of hydrogen inside the Sun is converted into helium every second.

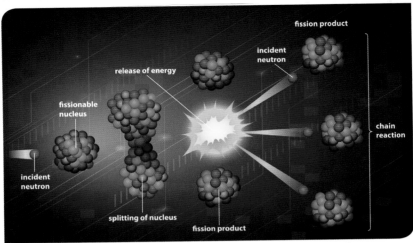

▲ *Nuclear fission results in the splitting of big nuclei into smaller ones.*

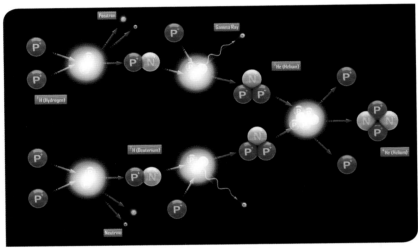

▲ *Nuclear fusion is the opposite reaction of fission.*

▲ *Nuclear power plants have to be operated safely to avoid dangers.*

Nuclear Reactor

Nuclear power plants consist of one or more nuclear reactors that use the mechanism of nuclear fission on heavy atoms like uranium and plutonium to produce nuclear energy. The energy results in a lot of heat that is used to convert water into steam, and the steam is used for powering electric turbines to produce electricity.

Nuclear energy generation has its advantages and disadvantages. It does not cause pollution and is more energy-efficient than many other fuel sources. Producing nuclear energy does not cause air pollution.

However, building a nuclear power plant is very expensive because many safety features have to be constructed for safe handling of the radioactive material. Any accidents in the nuclear plant can cause large-scale destruction and endanger for lives. The Chernobyl nuclear accident that occurred in Russia in 1986 is one of the worst nuclear disasters in history. Presently, there are 451 nuclear reactors across different parts of the world, contributing about 5 percent of the total global energy produced.

Background Radiation

We are surrounded by background radiation. The cosmic rays from outer space and artificially constructed sources of nuclear radiation (from weapons and reactor accidents) can cause physical damage to living tissues. The quantum of damage and risk depends on the dosage of the radiation. Radiation is measured in units called sieverts.

◀ *Earth is surrounded by cosmic radiation but is protected by its magnetic field and atmosphere.*

Radioactive Contamination and Hazards

Close proximity or contact with radioactive elements is dangerous because of the ionising radiation they emit. The process of exposing an object to nuclear radiation is known as irradiation. An irradiated object cannot become radioactive. Usually the different parts of the body can tolerate about 0.15 to 0.5 sieverts of radiation without causing any considerable harmful effects.

Radioactive waste generated in nuclear reactors is disposed of with great care and precaution.

▲ *Radioactive waste is stored and disposed of in special containers.*

Storage of Radioactive Materials

Radioactive isotopes as well as waste from nuclear reactors have to be stored in suitable containers. Usually, lead is the choice of material for containers. Lead provides protection against radiation mostly because it is dense and thick. Sometimes, steel containers with concrete casing can also be used as an alternative for lead. For an additional degree of safety, the materials are stored in rooms or spaces with locks or limited access. The radioactivity symbol is prominently displayed to warn people from handling the containers.

▲ *A Geiger counter is used for checking radiation levels of radioisotopes.*

A Geiger counter is a device used for detecting and measuring radiation from radioactive materials. People who work in such laboratories routinely assess the radiation levels using this device as a safety precaution.

The best method, currently used, for the disposal of radioactive waste is to dispose of it deep underground in specially designed facilities. This is known as geological disposal and is done to ensure that the radioactive waste does not contaminate groundwater or soil.

Forces

Force is defined as an interaction such as a push or a pull with an object which, when not opposed by anything else, will change an object's motion. While constructing machines and mega projects, engineers analyse the effect of force and design accordingly.

▲ *A footballer kicking a ball is an example of contact force*

Contact and Noncontact Forces

All forces between objects are contact or noncontact forces. Contact forces are physically in contact with the object, while noncontact forces are physically separated. There are many different kinds of forces that one can observe.

A few examples of contact forces include friction, air resistance and tension. Gravitational force and electrostatic force are examples of noncontact forces.

▲ *Gravity is a noncontact force that pulls any object toward the ground.*

Gravity

An object's weight is the force exerted by gravity on the object. The force from gravity is the result of the gravitational field around the Earth. The weight of an object depends on the gravitational field strength with respect to the object's location. An object's weight is directly proportional to its mass.

Weight can be calculated using the formula:

W = m g

W – Weight
m – Mass of the object
g – Gravitational field strength

Types of Force

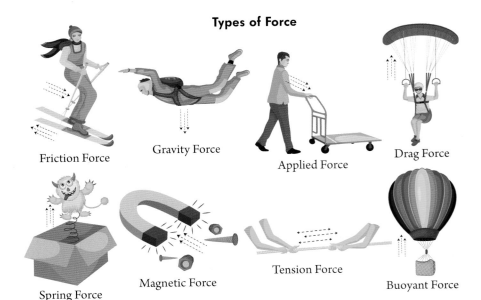

Friction Force

Gravity Force

Applied Force

Drag Force

Spring Force

Magnetic Force

Tension Force

Buoyant Force

Resultant Force

An object can be acted upon by a number of forces at the same time. If a single force could have the same effect as the sum total of all other forces, then such a force is called a resultant force. A resultant force can be equal to many other forces acting together. On the other hand, the resultant force can be zero when the net total forces cancel out.

Work and Moment

When the application of a force causes an object to move across a certain distance, then work is said to be done.

Work done = Force x Distance moved

W = F s

W – Work
F – Force
s – Distance from original position

Work is measured in joules. One joule of work is said to be done when the application of a force of one newton is applied to an object and it is displaced by a distance of one metre.

Sometimes, a force or a group of forces may cause an object to rotate instead of moving. The turning effect of the force is called the moment.

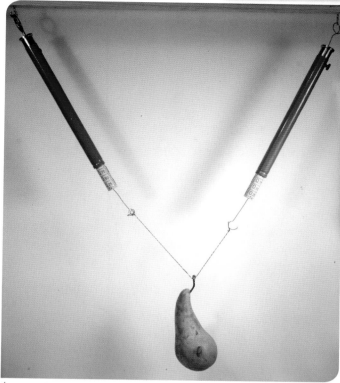

▲ *When two or more forces act on a body, they cancel out or add up.*

◄ *Work is the result of force applied and distance traveled.*

Fact File

Irrespective of type, all forces exert a pull or a push on an object.

Atmospheric Pressure

The atmosphere is a thin, protective layer around the Earth. It has many layers, and with increasing altitude, the air becomes less dense. The number of air molecules above a surface decreases with an increase in height. The force applied by the entire body of air in the atmosphere is known as atmospheric pressure or barometric pressure, which can be measured using a device called a barometer.

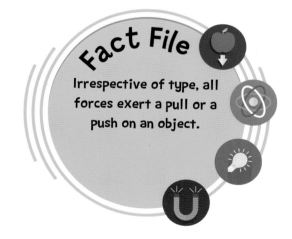

◄ *A barometer is used for measuring atmospheric pressure.*

Motion

Even as you observe your surroundings, you will realise that most things you see are in motion. Even though we do not sense it, Earth is hurtling across space around the Sun at an incredible speed. Motion is an important phenomenon in the universe and different kinds of forces are responsible for motion.

Types of Motion

Motion can be classified as simple or complex. Simple motion consists of an object moving along a straight line or a pendulum swinging to and fro at a fairly constant rate.

Some of the common types of motion include:

Linear motion: An object moving along a straight line is said to be in linear motion. This is one of the most fundamental types of motion. A moving object, when not subject to any external force, will continue to move in a straight line with constant velocity.

▲ *The movement of a bowling ball is an example of linear motion.*

▲ *A Ferris wheel exhibits rotary motion.*

Circular motion: The movement of an object in a circular path. The orbit of a planet around the Sun is a classic example of circular motion.

Rotary motion: The rotation of an object around a fixed point is rotary motion. A Ferris wheel and the rotation of a planet around its axis are examples of this type of motion.

▲ *The action of a saw is a reciprocating motion.*

Random motion: Movement of any object that is not easy to predict, fixed or regular, is called random motion.

Reciprocating motion: The to-and-fro rhythmic movement of an object, like a saw cutting wood, is known as reciprocating motion.

Oscillation: The movement of an object from one end of its central position to the other end and then back to the central position and further on is known as oscillation. The pendulum exhibits oscillatory motion.

▲ *This device, Newton's cradle, exhibits oscillatory motion.*

Measuring Motion

Distance travelled by an object is how far it travels. Displacement, measures the distance travelled in a straight line from one point to another along with the direction. Speed is measured as the rate at which an object travels. No object ever travels at a constant speed, and it varies continuously.

The speed of a person depends on the terrain, fitness level, age and other factors. Different activities are done at different speeds. On average, a person can walk a distance of 1.5 metres per second, run 3 metres per second, or cycle at 6 metres per second.

Even the speed of wind or sound is never constant. The speed of sound in air versus its speed in water varies.

Speed can be measured using the formula:

$$Speed = \frac{Distance\ Travelled}{Time\ Taken}$$

Velocity is a measure of how fast an object moves in a particular direction. The rate of change of velocity is called acceleration.

Speed is How Fast you are Traveling ...

This Car is Traveling at a Speed of 20m/s

Speed is a Scalar Quantity that Refers to "How Fast an Object is Moving"

Velocity is Speed in a given Direction ...

This Car is Traveling at a Velocity of 20m/s East

Velocity is a Vector Quantity that Refers to "the Rate at which an Object Changes its Position"

Fact File

All the galaxies, including our Milky Way, are moving away from each other at tremendous speed.

Speed denotes how fast one travels, while velocity also gives direction.

Gravity and Motion

Close to the Earth's surface, any object that is falling freely is under the influence of Earth's gravitational force and has an acceleration of 9.8 metres/second. If a body is falling through a fluid, it will initially accelerate due to the effect of gravity and gradually slow down (or decelerate) due to the buoyant force of the liquid that acts upward, in the opposite direction of gravity.

Gravitational force acts on a body and pulls it toward the Earth.

Newton's Laws

Isaac Newton was one of the most influential scientists in history and made major contributions in the understanding of important physical phenomena, especially gravity and planetary motion. He set forth a set of three laws to describe the relation between mass and motion.

Newton's Law of Motion

Newton put together a set of three laws of motion that make up the foundation of mechanics: the study of motion of objects in the universe. The laws were developed to predict and describe the relationship between an object and the forces acting upon it, and how the object's motion is affected by the forces.

Isaac Newton compiled the laws in his work *Principia Mathematica*, first published in 1687. Newton's laws have been observed and experimentally verified for over two centuries.

Newton's First Law of Motion

"Every object continues in its state of rest or uniform motion in a straight line unless it is forced to change the state due to the action of external forces."

The tendency of an object to remain unchanged at rest or in motion is called inertia. The state of inertia is affected only when one or more forces act on the object. Even if there are multiple forces acting on an object, the object can continue in its state of inertia if the forces cancel each other out.

▲ *Isaac Newton was among the most influential physicists in the world*

Newton's First Law of Motion

An object at rest stays at rest.

An object acted upon by a balanced force stays at rest.

An object acted upon by an unbalanced force changes speed and direction.

An object at rest stays at rest.

An object acted upon by an unbalanced force changes speed and direction.

An object in motion stays in motion.

An object acted upon by an unbalanced force changes speed and direction.

Astronauts sometimes travel to the International Space Station to conduct repairs or routine maintenance. They can place the tools beside them in space and the tools will stay, without falling down or moving away. This is because there is no force acting on them (such as gravity) to interfere with their state of rest. Similarly, if the tool is pushed away, it will continue moving unless stopped by some external force.

Newton's Second Law

"The greater the mass of an object, the more force it takes to accelerate it."

Acceleration of an object is the effect of some force acting on it. It is inversely proportional to the object's mass. The greater the mass of the object that is being accelerated, the more force that is needed to accelerate it. Newton's second law of motion gives the relationship between force, acceleration, and mass through a mathematical formula:

Resultant Force = Mass x Acceleration

Fact File

Newton's laws of motion do not apply on small-scale objects like atoms.

Newton's Second Law of Motion

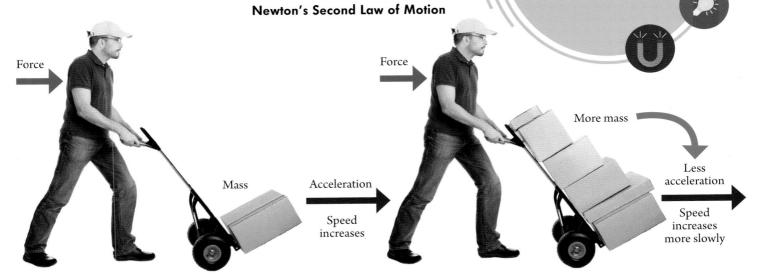

Force — Mass — Acceleration — Speed increases

Force — More mass — Less acceleration — Speed increases more slowly

Newton's Third Law

"For every action, there is an equal and opposite reaction."

In every interaction, a pair of forces acts on the two bodies or objects. The size of the force of the first object is equivalent to that of the second object acting in the opposite direction. According to this law, all forces come in pairs.

A rocket that is preparing to be launched into space pushes against the ground, applying the force using its powerful engines. The ground applies an equal and opposite force to push the rocket away from it in the upward direction.

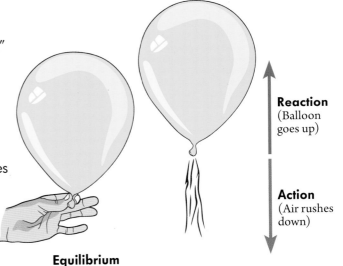

Reaction
(Balloon goes up)

Action
(Air rushes down)

Equilibrium

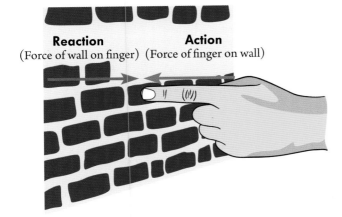

Reaction
(Force of wall on finger)

Action
(Force of finger on wall)

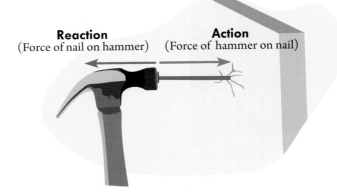

Reaction
(Force of nail on hammer)

Action
(Force of hammer on nail)

Physics of Driving

All moving objects, such as vehicles, are subject to different laws of physics. Many factors are involved in the driving of a vehicle—gravity, friction, inertia, potential energy, and kinetic energy. These factors decide how the vehicle moves and interacts with objects around it.

Driving Uphill and Downhill

The two major factors acting upon a moving vehicle are gravity and traction. Gravity is a force that pulls all objects closer to the Earth. Friction is a force that resists motion when two materials slide against each other.

Traction is caused due to friction between the road and the weight of the car upon the tires. Traction is essential because it is the interaction between the road and the tires that enables a driver to steer the car.

Gravity can aid or hinder a vehicle depending on whether it is being driven uphill or downhill. When a driver drives a vehicle uphill, gravity works against it, as its natural tendency is to pull it down toward the Earth. The driver needs to accelerate the vehicle more to work against the gravitational force. While driving downhill, gravity aids the vehicle instead of being a hindrance. Gravity will enable the vehicle to move faster.

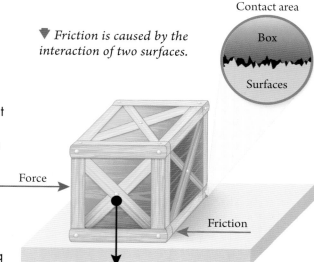

▼ *Friction is caused by the interaction of two surfaces.*

Contact area

Box

Surfaces

Force

Friction

Gravity

Braking

All vehicles are designed for acceleration. It is important for them to be equipped with a braking mechanism that enables their movement to come to a halt by gradually slowing them down. The brakes slow down a moving vehicle by using friction between the wheel and another object. When a force is applied to the vehicle's brakes, the frictional force between the wheels and the braking mechanism reduces the kinetic energy of the vehicle.

The greater the speed of the vehicle, the higher the braking force has to be to bring it to a halt. Consequently, the greater the braking force, the larger the deceleration will be. Large and sudden decelerations can often cause the brakes to heat up and even lose control.

A driver's reaction time is defined as the time taken to respond to a particular situation. As this is a variable factor, the reaction time varies greatly from person to person. Also, different factors can affect the reaction time of an individual.

The stopping distance of a vehicle is calculated as the sum of the distance travelled by the vehicle during the driver's reaction time and the distance traveled after applying the brakes, also called the braking distance.

Potential Energy and Momentum of a Vehicle

When a bicycle is on top of a hill, it possesses potential energy due to gravity. The stored potential energy is converted into kinetic energy while riding it downhill.

The force of a moving vehicle is called its momentum. The vehicle's momentum depends on its weight and speed. A driver doubles a car's momentum when he increases its speed from 10 miles per hour to 20. When a speeding vehicle is stopped, the momentum is overcome by the friction of the brakes applied between the wheels and the road.

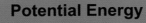
Potential and kinetic energy interconvert when a person rides uphill and downhill.

▲ *Brakes slow down a moving vehicle.*

▲ *A fast-moving vehicle needs a higher braking force to stop.*

Fact File
Early cars achieved speeds in the range of 10 miles per hour. The fastest car today can reach a speed of 270.4 miles per hour!

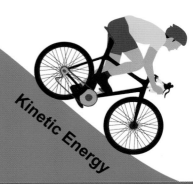

Energy IN   **Potential Energy**   **Energy OUT**

Kinetic Energy   Kinetic Energy

Magnetism

People have known about magnetism since ancient times. Lodestones that were capable of attracting iron objects were used for navigation because of their ability to always align toward the north.

Principle of Magnetism

Originally, the domain theory was used to explain magnetism. According to the theory, a strongly magnetic substance has tiny pockets called domains. There is no magnetism when the domains are arranged randomly. However, when the domains align in the same direction, the net effect produces a magnetic field.

With a better understanding of atoms and their constituents, scientists identified that magnetism arose as a result of the rapidly spinning motion of electrons. Since electrons have electric charge, the spinning motion generated a magnetic field. The sum total of the magnetic fields generated by all the electrons in a material confers its magnetic property.

▲ *Lodestones were used for navigation in ancient times.*

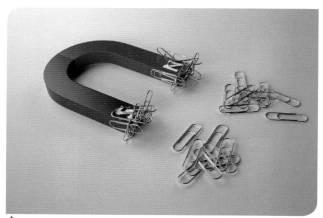
▲ *Ferromagnetic materials are used for making permanent magnets.*

Types of Magnetism

Every object or material on Earth exhibits one of the three types of magnetism: ferromagnetism, paramagnetism, and diamagnetism.

Ferromagnetism: Is considered the strongest form of magnetism and means 'magnetic like iron.' Ferromagnetism is exhibited by a few elements such as iron and rare earth metals. They can be magnetised when brought in close proximity to a magnetic field. They remain magnetised even after the magnetic field is removed. Heating or striking a ferromagnetic material can make it lose some or all of its magnetic properties.

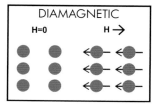 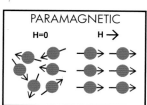 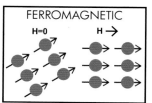
▲ *Magnetism is conferred by the direction of alignment of spinning electrons.*

Paramagnetism: Is a weak form of magnetism exhibited by certain elements like gold, copper and aluminium. A paramagnetic material, when suspended from a string, aligns parallel to the Earth's magnetic field. Paramagnetism is so weak that it is nearly unobservable. Like ferromagnetism, paramagnetism diminishes upon heating.

Diamagnetism: Nonmetals and most other materials exhibit diamagnetism. Diamagnetic materials repel magnetic fields. At the atomic level, diamagnetism is caused by the net spin of electrons cancelling out and becoming zero. When a diamagnetic material is brought into a magnetic field, it aligns opposite to the direction of the magnetic field. Pyrolytic carbon is a material that is so strongly diamagnetic that it is repelled by neodymium magnets.

▲ *Strongly diamagnetic material gets repelled from a strong magnet.*

Magnetic Field

A magnetic field is the space around a magnet where its magnetism is the strongest. Generally, the magnetic force is strongest near the poles of a magnet. Two magnets, when brought in contact, exert magnetic force on each other, which could result in attraction or repulsion. The magnetic force is an example of a noncontact force.

▲ *Two magnets can attract or repel each other.*

Fact File

Magnets are an important component of laptop and desktop computers.

▲ *Iron filings can be used to demonstrate the magnetic lines of force.*

A permanent magnet always has its own magnetic field. An induced magnet is any magnetic material that becomes a magnet when placed within the magnetic field. It loses all or most of its magnetic properties when moved away from the influence of the magnetic field. The magnetic lines of force emanate from the north pole and converge at the south pole, and reconnect inside the magnet. The lines of force never intersect.

When a magnet is rubbed over magnetic materials like iron or nickel, it can magnetise the material. Magnets can lose their magnetic properties if heated.

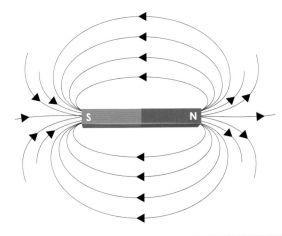

Northern and Southern Lights

The northern lights phenomenon, or aurora borealis, is caused by the interaction of charged particles with Earth's magnetic field. It can be viewed in Alaska and Iceland. The southern lights, also called aurora australis, is observed in New Zealand, Tasmania and Antarctica.

These phenomenal displays are produced when highly charged electrons from the solar wind interact with Earth's magnetic lines of force. When the electrons enter the Earth's atmosphere, they interact with the nitrogen and oxygen present in it. The colour of the lights depend on which gas the electrons interact with.

▲ *The northern lights are colourful displays of lights caused by Earth's magnetic field.*

Properties of Magnets

Any material capable of producing a magnetic field is called a magnet. The unique properties of magnets are valuable in understanding the phenomenon of magnetism, and also find applications in a variety of fields.

Nature of Magnets

Natural magnets have two poles, a north pole and a south pole. No matter how many times the magnet is cut or divided, it will always have two poles. Just like electric charges, like magnetic poles repel and unlike poles attract. The north pole and the south pole attract each other. Even circular and disc magnets have two poles, one on either side or at two ends.

▲ All magnets have a north and south pole.

▲ William Gilbert suggested that Earth was like a giant magnet.

Earth: A Giant Magnet

A magnetic compass consists of a thin needle made of magnet that can align itself to the Earth's North Pole no matter where one stands. This phenomenon occurs only because the Earth itself behaves like a giant magnet. The Earth is rich in magnetic material like iron that gives it its magnetic properties.

The first person to suggest that the Earth behaves like a gigantic magnet was William Gilbert, in 1600. The Earth's magnetic field stretches out into space for thousands of kilometres and is known as the magnetosphere. The magnetosphere plays a crucial role in protecting us from the harmful cosmic radiation and charged particles from the Sun.

▼ Earth has a magnetic field that extends for thousands of kilometres into space.

Magnetic Fields in the Solar System

The magnetic field of any object is measured in units called teslas. Earth has a considerably strong gravitational field, but its magnetic field is surprisingly weak. To give a comparison, an ordinary bar magnet has a magnetic field strength at least 100–1,000 times stronger than that of Earth. The strongest magnets ever manufactured in laboratories can have a magnetic field up to 900,000 times stronger than the Earth's magnetic field.

The moon does not exhibit magnetism because it is not made up of a sufficient percentage of any elements that have magnetic properties. The Sun and the larger planets like Jupiter, Saturn, Uranus and Neptune have a much stronger magnetic field.

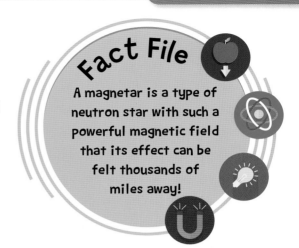

Fact File

A magnetar is a type of neutron star with such a powerful magnetic field that its effect can be felt thousands of miles away!

Types of Magnets

Some of the most powerful permanent magnets are made by combining different magnetic materials. The four types of permanent magnets are:

1. Neodymium Iron Boron (NdFeB) Magnets: These magnets are made with an alloy of neodymium, iron and boron.

The NdFeB magnets can be made to be small and compact yet very powerful. On the downside, they tend to be brittle and have very low resistance to corrosion unless coated with a protective layer. These magnets are generally coated with iron, nickel or gold and are used in many different applications.

2. Samarium Cobalt (SmCo) Magnets: They are made using an alloy of samarium and cobalt. Like the NdFeB variety, SmCo magnets are also very strongly magnetic with the added advantages of being resistant to temperature and oxidation—and hence they are very durable. However, SmCo magnets are very expensive and tend to break easily. Both NdFeB and SmCo magnets are made from rare earth metals.

3. Alnico Magnets: The magnets are named from the first letters of the main components—aluminium, nickel and cobalt. Unlike the rare earth magnets, these magnets can be stripped of their magnetic properties very easily.

▲ *Neodymium iron boron magnets.*

▲ *Inexpensive and easily available ceramic magnets.*

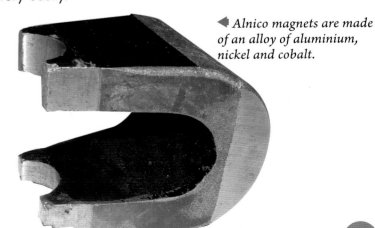

◄ *Alnico magnets are made of an alloy of aluminium, nickel and cobalt.*

4. Ceramic Magnets: Also called ferrite magnets, they are made of iron oxide and barium or strontium carbonate. These magnets have strong magnetic properties and are cheap and easy to produce, and hence are commonly used.

Electromagnetism

Electricity and magnetism were originally considered to be different and unrelated phenomena. The possibility of electricity and magnetism being interrelated was proposed and verified in the nineteenth century. The term 'electromagnetism' refers to the interaction of electric and magnetic fields.

Observation of Electromagnetism

In the year 1820, Hans Christian Oersted, a Danish physicist, discovered electromagnetism quite by accident. While switching a battery on and off, he noticed deflection in a magnetic needle placed nearby. It helped him identify that magnetic fields radiate in all directions from a wire carrying current.

▲ *Hans Christian Oersted discovered that electricity and magnetism were related.*

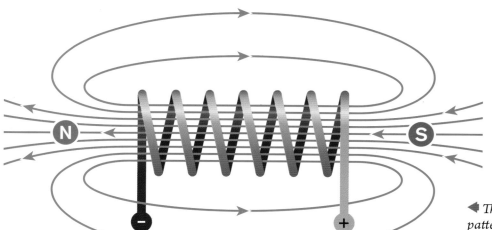

◀ *The electromagnetic field pattern around a coil of wire.*

Electromagnet

A naturally magnetic substance like iron, nickel, or cobalt can be converted into an electromagnet by wrapping it tightly with coils of wire and connecting the two ends of a wire to a battery. This electromagnet temporarily acquires magnetic properties and will retain it as long as it is connected to electricity. The more coils present, the stronger the magnetic effect.

Electromagnets and Permanent Magnets

A permanent magnet has fixed north and south poles that cannot be altered. The north-south polarity of electromagnets can be altered as and when necessary by changing the direction of the current in the coil.

Industrial-scale electromagnets are very powerful and can produce magnetic fields stronger than permanent magnets. The biggest advantage of an electromagnet is that it is possible to adjust its magnetic force strength by altering the amount of current that flows through it or the number of turns of wire.

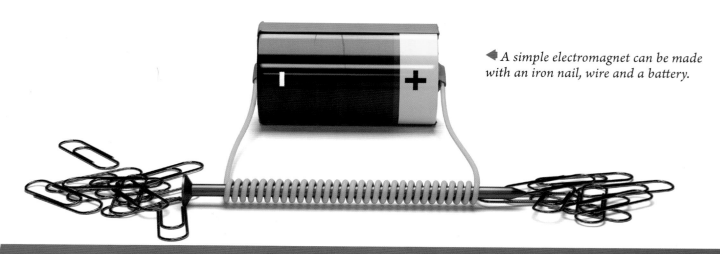

◀ *A simple electromagnet can be made with an iron nail, wire and a battery.*

Mechanism of Electromagnetism

Inside a wire, the flow of electrons results in the formation of a magnetic field. The magnetic field lines are always oriented in a direction perpendicular to the flow of electricity. The magnetic field force created by an electromagnet is also sometimes called the magnetomotive force. The strength of this force is determined by the number of coils and the amount of current passing through an electromagnet.

A cylindrical coil of wire acting as a magnet when carrying electric current is called a solenoid. A solenoid can achieve good magnetic field strength owing to its coils and shape. The magnetic field created within a solenoid is uniform and strong.

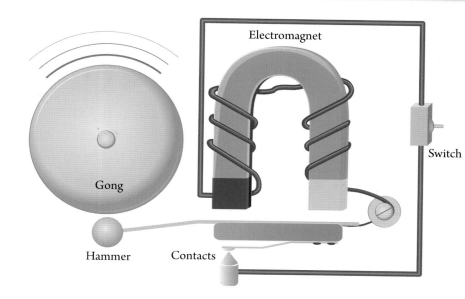

▲ *An electric bell is a device that works on the principle of electromagnetism.*

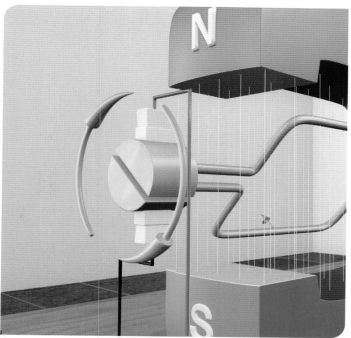

▲ *The generator effect shows that a moving electric wire in a fixed magnetic field produces current.*

Generator Effect

In the same way as an electric current flowing through a wire generates a magnetic field, the movement of an electric wire inside a magnet's magnetic field generates an electric current. This is called the generator effect. There is no physical contact between the magnet and the wire. The electric current is induced by the magnetic field.

Electromagnetic Induction

In the presence of a changing magnetic field through a current-carrying conductor, an electromotive force is generated. This process is called electromagnetic induction. Many devices like transformers, motors, and generators work on this principle.

Fact File

William Sturgeon, an English physicist, produced the first usable electromagnet in 1825.

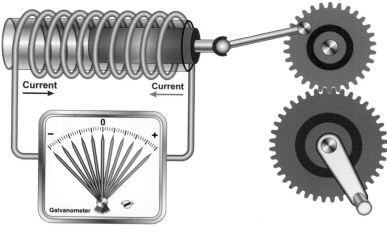

▲ *Electromagnetic induction involves a fixed conductor and changing magnetic field.*

Applications of Electromagnetism

Electromagnets have numerous applications such as the manufacture of generators, motors, transformers, loudspeakers, and powerful lifting devices. They are used in various fields of engineering and technology and are indispensable in today's world of communication and advancement.

Electric Motors

An electric motor is generally equipped with magnets, a rotating shaft, and wires. It operates on the rotation produced by a current-carrying coil of wire in a magnetic field. The rotational energy of a motor can be used for powering many different electric appliances like food processors, water pumps, vacuum cleaners and fans.

▲ Copper wires, a rotating shaft and magnets are the major components of a motor.

Motors are also used in loudspeakers and microphones. The motor converts current variations in the electric circuits into pressure vibrations of sound waves. Microphones do just the opposite—they work on the principle of generator effect and convert pressure variations into electric current.

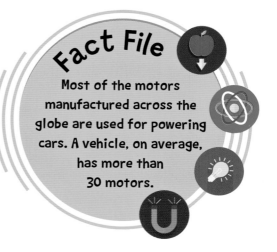

◀ In a food processor, a motor helps power the rotating blades attached to its shaft.

Other Uses of Electromagnets

1. Powerful electromagnets are used in scientific analysis instruments like spectrometers and particle accelerators. In a particle accelerator, electromagnets are employed for steering and focusing beams of particles traveling through a vacuum tube.

▲ *Maglev trains achieve high speeds impossible in regular trains.*

2. The ultrafast Maglev trains work on the principle of magnetic levitation. The trains, instead of running over regular tracks, instead levitate in the air due to repulsion of electromagnets in the train's underside and the guideway. Maglev trains are able to achieve very high speeds because the lack of contact with any surface greatly cuts down friction.

▲ *Magnetic separators often employ electromagnets.*

3. Strong permanent magnets, as well as electromagnets, are used in magnetic separators. Separators are employed in junkyards to separate metals from other common junk for recycling.

4. Power transformers also work on the principle of electromagnetic induction to increase or decrease voltage of the current transmitted from power lines.

▲ *Interior of a particle accelerator that employs electromagnets.*

5. Electromagnets are important components of medical imaging devices such as magnetic resonance imaging (MRI) machines. The MRI's magnet is equipped in the hollow tube through which the patient enters. It generates magnetic fields much more powerful than that of the Earth's field.

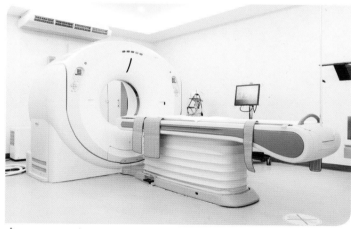

▲ *MRI machines produce powerful magnetic fields.*

6. An induction cooker consists of a ceramic plate equipped with an electromagnetic coil and works on the principle of electromagnetic induction to produce electricity and heat in the presence of a magnetic field.

▲ *Induction stoves work on the principle of electromagnetic induction.*

Waves

Any regular and recurring phenomenon is called a wave. A wave is defined by its properties like wavelength, frequency and speed. Waves help transfer energy and carry information. Modern technology has enabled us not only to understand better about waves like electromagnetic radiation but also to make the best use of them.

Transverse and Longitudinal Waves

Waves come in different forms. All waves have certain characteristic features as well as others that distinguish them from one another. Commonly, waves are classified into two types: transverse and longitudinal. Transverse and longitudinal waves are classified based on the direction of their movement.

▲ *Ripples forming in water are an example of transverse waves.*

A transverse wave is a type of wave that travels in a direction perpendicular to the movement of the particles in a particular medium. The ripples forming on the surface of a pond after a pebble is dropped are an example of transverse waves. The waves form in a direction perpendicular to the movement of the pebble as it sinks down.

A longitudinal wave is a wave type that moves in a direction parallel to the movement of the particles. Sound waves traveling from the mouth of the speaker to the ears of a listener are an example of longitudinal waves.

Apart from longitudinal and transverse waves, there are also surface waves that travel along large surfaces such as oceans. A surface wave consists of particles moving in circular motion.

Apart from direction, waves are also classified based on their ability to transmit energy in a vacuum or empty space. Based on this factor, mechanical waves are those waves that cannot transmit energy in a vacuum. Sound waves, an example of mechanical waves, cannot travel in a vacuum and need a medium to travel. Electromagnetic waves, produced by the vibration of charged particles, can transmit energy in a vacuum.

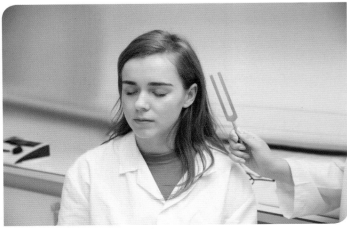

▲ *The sound from a tuning fork to a listener travels as longitudinal waves.*

Transverse Wave

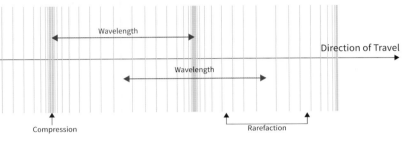

Longitudinal Wave

▲ Transverse and longitudinal waves have different properties.

Wave Properties

A wave motion can be described in terms of amplitude, frequency and wavelength. A wave's amplitude is its maximum displacement away from its undisturbed position. A wave's frequency is calculated as the number of waves crossing a certain reference point in a second. The wavelength is the distance from a point on one wave to an equivalent point in the wave adjacent to it. The speed of a wave is the speed at which energy is transferred when a wave moves through a medium. The highest point of a wave is called the crest and the lowest point is called the trough. A wave can be made to oscillate in just one direction. This property is known as polarisation. Only transverse waves can be polarised.

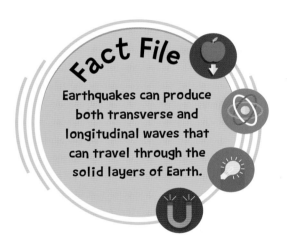

Fact File

Earthquakes can produce both transverse and longitudinal waves that can travel through the solid layers of Earth.

Waves exhibit different behaviour when they encounter different mediums and obstacles, or come in contact with other waves.

Reflection: When a wave hits a medium that acts as a barrier, it returns to the original medium. This is known as reflection.

Refraction: The change in direction that a wave encounters when it passes from one medium to another is called refraction.

Diffraction: When a wave travels through a medium, it can sometimes bend when it comes into contact with an obstacle or is forced to pass through a tiny slit.

Absorption: When waves come into contact with the atoms of a medium, the atoms vibrate and absorb energy from the waves.

Scattering: Light and sound scatter or deviate from their path of travel when they encounter small particles and molecules in their path.

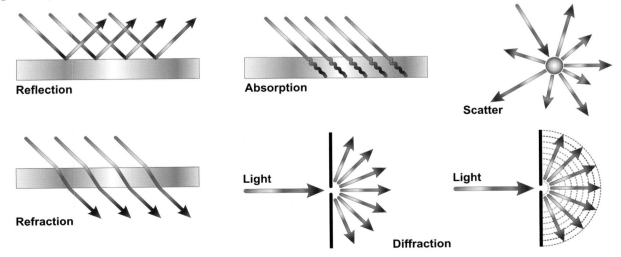

▲ Waves exhibit different properties under varied conditions.

Electromagnetic Radiation

Electromagnetic radiation exists in the form of waves that can transfer energy from the source to anything capable of absorbing it. Electromagnetic waves exist as a continuous spectrum ranging from short to long wavelengths.

Electromagnetic Wave Types

The electromagnetic spectrum consists of different types of waves.

Radio Waves: These have the longest wavelength, reaching about 10^3 nanometres (nm), and are used for transmitting radio and television broadcasts as well as mobile phone communications. They are also used for remote sensing and radar systems for navigation. Radio waves have the lowest energy levels in the spectrum.

Microwaves: Like radio waves, microwaves are useful for broadcasting information through space and remote sensing. They are very efficient at transmitting information because microwaves can even penetrate through clouds and rain. They are also useful for producing heat and are used in microwave ovens.

▲ Satellite dishes capture radio waves for radio and television broadcasting.

Infrared Radiation: Can be released as heat and bounced back like visible light. In fact, infrared radiation has many similarities to visible light. Infrared sensors are useful for collecting thermal energy data and have applications in military surveillance. Infrared radiation can also be used for predicting weather conditions.

Visible Light: This is the only portion of the electromagnetic spectrum that is visible to humans, extending from 390 to 780 nm. Visible light splits into a variety of colours each representing a particular wavelength.

▲ Infrared radiation can provide thermal energy data of objects and living things.

Colour Region	Wavelength (nm)
Violet	380–435
Blue	435–500
Cyan	500–520
Green	520–565
Yellow	565–590
Orange	590–625
Red	625–740

Ultraviolet Radiation: With wavelengths in the range of 10–400 nm, it lies midway between visible light and X-rays. It is emitted from the Sun, constituting about 10 percent of the total light coming out. Long-wavelength UV radiation is not considered ionising radiation, but it is still capable of producing a chemical reaction that causes glowing and fluorescence. Short-wavelength UV radiation is harmful because it can cause DNA mutation and cancer.

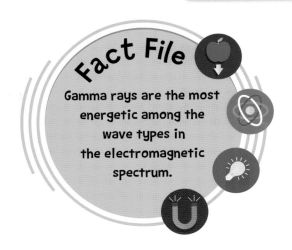

Gamma rays are the most energetic among the wave types in the electromagnetic spectrum.

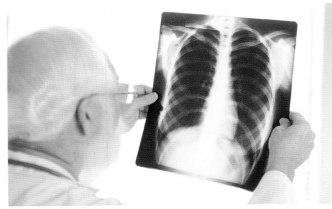

▲ *X-rays are used widely for diagnosis of problems within the body.*

X-rays: They have wavelengths in the range of 0.01–10 nm, and a high penetrating ability. Hence, X-rays are used in photographing bones and internal structures within the body. High doses of X-rays can cause cancer and other harmful effects.

Gamma Rays: They have the shortest wavelength at around 0.001 nm and highest energy in the electromagnetic spectrum that arises from the decay of atomic nuclei. Gamma rays can only be shielded using heavy materials such as lead or concrete. In the universe, gamma ray bursts can occur during the explosion of a star. Gamma radiation dose is measured in sieverts and can cause significant harm in doses beyond the recommended limit.

▼ *When a star explodes, it can result in gamma ray bursts.*

The Solar System

People have been fascinated by the features in the sky and have been attempting to seek answers about them. In the past hundred or so years, we have seen remarkable progress in our understanding of the universe.

Solar System

Our Solar System comprises a single star (the Sun) and the eight planets as well as their satellites, dwarf planets and asteroids. The Solar System is merely a minuscule part of the much larger Milky Way galaxy with billions of other such star systems.

The planets in the order of proximity to the Sun are: Mercury, Venus, Earth, Mars, Jupiter, Saturn, Uranus and Neptune. Next to the Sun, Jupiter is the biggest object in the Solar System. Except Mercury and Venus, the other planets have one or more satellites also simply called moons.

Fact File

The Solar System is thought to have formed as a result of a supernova (explosion of a massive star) nearby.

▼ The Solar System consists of the Sun, the eight planets, their moons, dwarf planets, asteroids and comets.

Sun

Mercury

Venus

Earth

Mars

Jupiter

Saturn

Uranus

Neptune

Formation of the Solar System

The Sun and all the planets were formed from a cloud of gas and dust, known as a nebula. The swirling dust and gases were drawn together due to gravity after the explosion of a supernova nearby. The squeezed gases and dust spun fast, growing very hot and dense in the center and cooler around the edges.

Dust and gas began to accumulate into planets around the hot mass in the center. The icy matter in the cloud formed the cold planets, Uranus and Neptune. The light gases like hydrogen and helium floated farther from the hot mass, forming the large planets Jupiter and Saturn. The rocky material formed the four inner planets. The hot mass in the center grew hotter and eventually became a star. The remaining debris accumulated as asteroids. Most of the asteroids in the solar system are found as a belt between Mars and Jupiter.

Scientists have identified that the age of the Solar System is 4.6 billion years by studying meteorites that are considered to be remnants of the early phase of solar system formation.

▲ *The swirling gas and dust resulted in the formation of the sun and planets*

Orbital Motion

The curved path taken by any object around a star or a planet is called an orbit. The planets travel around the Sun in elliptical orbits. The planets around the Sun are subject to gravity. Gravity is a force that acts between two objects with mass. The Sun, as a massive body, exerts its gravitational pull on the planets.

The planets do not get pulled toward the Sun because they are already in motion in a direction perpendicular or sideways to the Sun's gravitational pull. The forces balance out and the planets remain in their orbits, without flying out of orbit or getting pulled into the Sun and getting burned.

It is a similar principle that keeps a natural satellite such as Earth's Moon orbiting the Earth without collapsing into the Earth's surface or moving away completely.

Moon

Earth

Artificial Satellites

Artificial satellites work on the fundamental principle of gravity. Isaac Newton predicted that if an object could be projected into space at sufficient speed, it could orbit the Earth. When launched at the right speed, the satellite would fall down at about the same rate as the Earth curves. This balance would enable the satellite to travel in a circular orbit around the Earth.

◀ *Artificial satellites orbit the Earth when launched at the right speed.*

Stars

There are countless numbers of stars in the universe, and millions in our Milky Way galaxy alone. A star typically starts its life from a cloud of dust and gas and passes through many stages over billions of years before it exhausts its energy and collapses back or explodes into dust.

▲ *A nebula is a massive cloud of gas and dust from which a star is formed.*

▲ *A brown dwarf is intermediate in size between a small star and a giant planet.*

Life Cycle of a Star

A star goes through a life cycle and its fate depends largely on its size. It begins its life as a cloud of dust and gas that is called a nebula.

The predominant gas found in this cloud is usually hydrogen. The gas cloud transforms into a protostar when the dust and gas begin to clump together due to gravity. This process is known as accretion.

The gravitational pull attracts more and more matter toward the core, increasing the temperature and pressure. When a particular temperature is reached in the protostar's core, the process of nuclear fusion begins.

Reaching the critical temperature is essential because if it fails to achieve the right temperature conditions, the protostar will never become a star. It might instead develop into a brown dwarf that is only a little bigger than the planet Jupiter, but much denser.

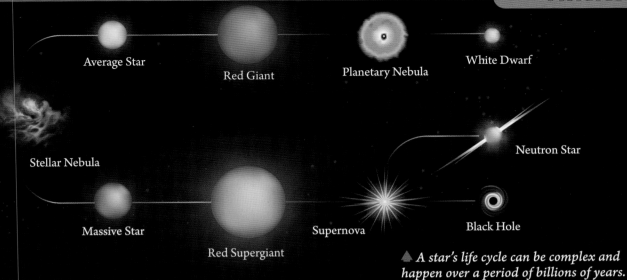

Average Star

Red Giant

Planetary Nebula

White Dwarf

Stellar Nebula

Neutron Star

Massive Star

Red Supergiant

Supernova

Black Hole

▲ *A star's life cycle can be complex and happen over a period of billions of years.*

The Sun is a yellow dwarf star. It generates energy by nuclear fusion, converting hydrogen into helium. The Sun's gravity keeps the hot gases within a confined space thus enabling fusion to occur continuously. This process remains in equilibrium as long as it has enough fuel to burn and produce heat. This period is called the main sequence of the star.

The Sun is already about 4.5–5 billion years old. It is expected to continue to exist mostly unchanged for another 5 billion years before the hydrogen runs out. With the hydrogen supply exhausted, the star's main sequence comes to an end. It starts to cool down and collapse for about 100 million years. The energy released due to the collapse heats up the star even more and it expands in size, becoming a red giant.

Afterward, the outer layers of the star explode away, leaving behind a small core, no bigger than the size of Earth. At this stage, the star is called a white dwarf. Its main constituents are carbon and oxygen. The white dwarfs lose their luminosity and fade away into space as black dwarfs. Most stars (up to 97 percent) face this fate in the Milky Way galaxy.

Large stars are hotter and brighter, but they do not exist for as long as a typical yellow dwarf. This is because large stars exhaust their fuel quickly. A star that is merely 20 times bigger than the Sun will burn out its fuel 36,000 times faster than the Sun and exist for a mere few million years.

◀ *A star becomes a white dwarf after losing its outer layers.*

Fact File

Most medium stars become white dwarfs, but massive stars go supernova.

Red Shift

Scientists have observed that the wavelength of light coming from distant galaxies increases. The more distant a galaxy is, the faster it is moving away. This phenomenon is known as red shift. It is proof for a rapidly expanding universe and also the Big Bang theory.

$$i\hbar\frac{\partial\psi}{\partial t}$$

$$(R_1 + R_3 + R_5 + r_{03}) - I_{k2}(R_3 + R_5)$$

$$+ R_3 + R_5 + r_{02}) - I_{k1}(R_3 + R_5)$$

$$6.6720*10^{-11} \ N*m^2/kg$$